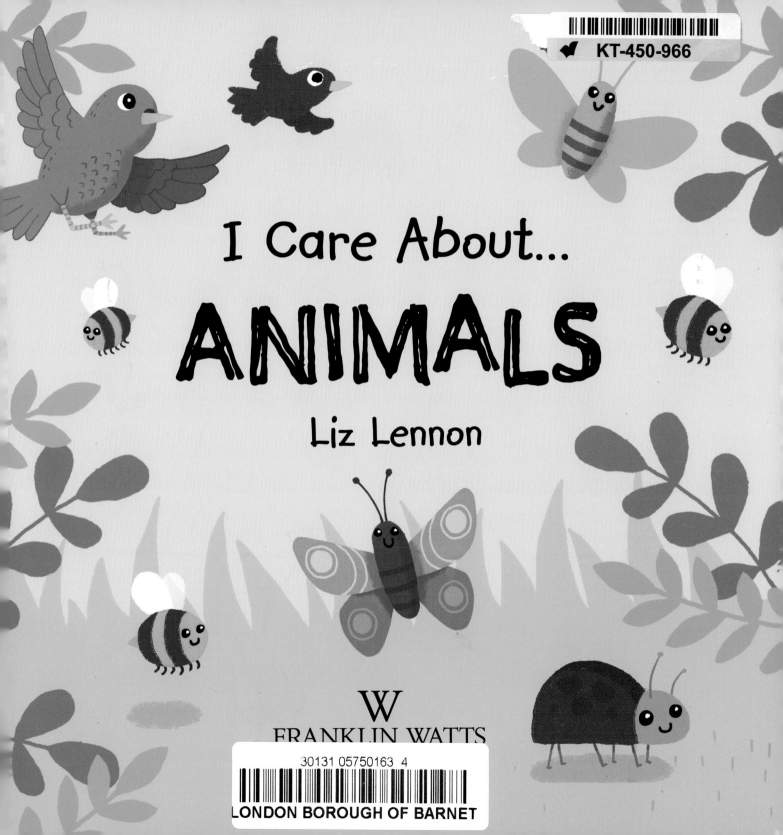

I Care About....

ANIMALS

Liz Lennon

W
FRANKLIN WATTS

Franklin Watts

First published in Great Britain in 2020 by The Watts Publishing Group
Text and illustrations copyright © The Watts Publishing Group, 2020

All rights reserved.

ISBN (HB): 978 1 4451 7105 0
ISBN (PB): 978 1 4451 7106 7

Printed in Dubai

Series Editor: Sarah Peutrill
Design: Collaborate
Illustration: Michael Buxton

Franklin Watts
An imprint of
Hachette Children's Group
Part of The Watts Publishing Group
Carmelite House
50 Victoria Embankment
London EC4Y 0DZ
An Hachette UK Company

www.hachette.co.uk
www.franklinwatts.co.uk

Contents

Animals big and small

The world is full of all sorts of animals.
The biggest animal is the blue whale. It is about the
length of two buses! Tiny animals live everywhere.
Some are so tiny you can't even see them.

All animals, big and small, are important. They make the planet a beautiful and exciting place to live. Many animals are important for protecting the planet too. Did you know that bees and other flying insects help plants to make seeds that grow into new plants?

Be kind

Animals are living things. Just as you are an animal who likes to be treated nicely, so do other animals. There are many types of places where you might meet an animal. You can see them in a garden, at the park, at a farm or the zoo. Wherever you are it's important to remember to be kind to animals.

Animal matching

Here are some animals. Can you match them with the places you might see them?

Earthworm	On a plant
Cow	In the soil
Crab	On a farm
Butterfly	On a beach

Be Kind to Animals

Looking after pets

Different pets need different things. If your family has a pet you will all need to learn what your pet needs. Your pet needs the right kind of food and place to sleep. Some pets need to have exercise. Some pets need to be kept safe from other animals.

Place the pets

Rabbits don't live in tanks! Can you put these pets back in their right homes?

If you meet someone else's pet, check with the owner before you touch it. Ask how and where you can stroke the pet.

Wild animals

There is a lot to learn about animals in the wild. It's fun to be curious about the natural world and the animals in it. Can you identify these different wild animals? Talk about the different things each of these animals needs to live. Are any of those things the same?

Draw your favourite animals

Learning to draw your favourite animals is fun. Look carefully at pictures first. Look at the different shapes of eyes, ears and tails. Check the number of legs. What patterns does it have on its skin or fur?

Outside your door

You might think the only interesting animals are in the ocean or in a rainforest. But there are plenty of interesting animals around you. Look under stones and leaves to find minibeasts. Watch out for busy ants on a hot day. See how a bee moves from flower to flower. Do you know what she's doing?

Meet the minibeasts

If you find a small animal when you're out and about, check with your grown-up before you touch it. Some small animals could be hurt if you touch them, and some can hurt you!

Make wildlife welcome

If you are lucky enough to have your own garden, there's some things you can do to help the wildlife in it. Ask your grown-up to leave a bit of garden to go wild. Hedgehogs like to move between gardens, so leave a hole in your fence for them to go through.

Build a bug hotel

Have you heard of a bug hotel? Bugs love a place with lots of holes and tiny places where they can set up home! You can build a bug hotel with your grown-up. It can be small – just a plant pot filled with bamboo sticks. Or if you have room and lots of materials, you could make a big one.

Out and about

You don't need a garden to see wildlife. Ask your grown-up if you can visit a park, woods or a pond to see what you can spot.

Go pond-dipping

Pond-dipping is a fun thing to do. You need a net with a long handle and a large tub or bucket. Fill the tub with pond water first. Sweep the net across the water and tip the contents into your tub. What can you see? Carefully put the contents of the tub back into the pond when you've had a good look.

Always be careful near water. Never go close without a grown-up.

Look at the map. Where do you think you are likely to see these animals?

Rabbit

Squirrel

Dragonfly

Frog

Fish

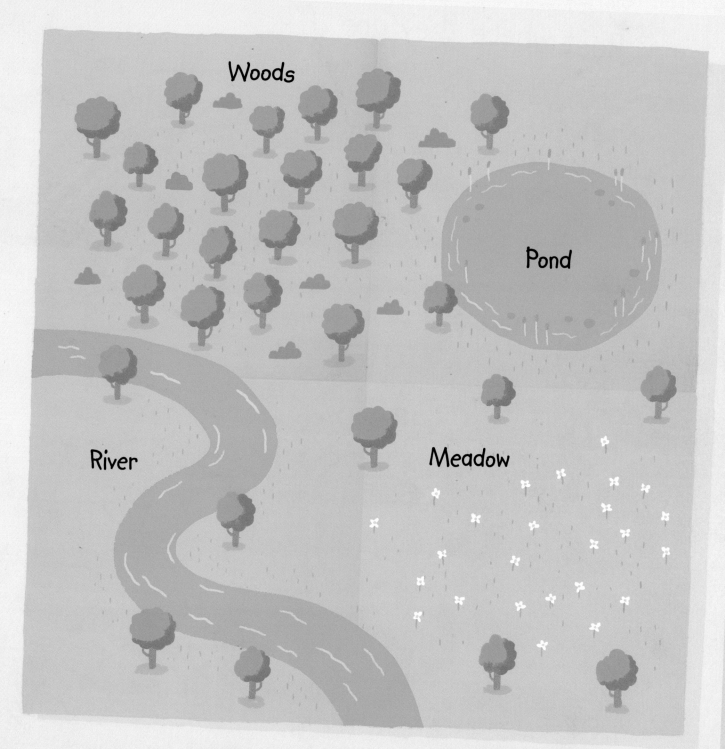

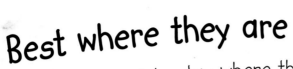

Best where they are

Animals in the wild want to stay where there are. They usually find the best place where there is food and shelter. Never feed human food to wild animals as it can hurt them.

Instead of taking animals home, take photos of them. Or you could take a nature-spotting notebook and draw some pictures. You might see some pets, too!

19

Tread carefully

When you're looking for nature, watch where you're walking. You never know what tiny animals are under your feet! In the woods, stick to paths.

If you want to spot shy animals, learn to walk quietly and make as little sound as possible. You are more likely to hear the animal sounds that way, and they are less likely to hear you and be frightened away!

Injured animals

If you *see* an injured animal, tell your grown-up. Never try to pick up a wild animal. If the animal needs help, your grown-up can call a vet.

Litter patrol

Litter harms wildlife. Animals eat food scraps, which are not good for them. Litter can also injure them. Never drop litter yourself. Always find a bin or take it home. With your grown-up, you can pick up litter and make your area safer for animals.

Habitats around the world

Animals live in different habitats around the world. There are different animals living in the big, blue ocean, hot and cold deserts and in woodlands and rainforests.

What are these animals and where do they live?

When habitats change or get smaller, the animals that live there can lose their home. There may be fewer of these animals or they may even die out altogether.

Endangered animals

Sadly, there are many animals that are in danger of dying out thanks to habitat loss, poaching and pollution. These include some of the biggest animals such as leopards, tigers and gorillas. Many more tiny animals are also endangered, including thousands of insects.

Help a charity

There are many charities that are working to protect animals and their homes. Speak to your grown-up if you have any ideas of how you can help a charity.

Dolphin

Tiger

Eagle

Elephant

Panda

Polar bear

Rhino

Gorilla

Did you know that these animals are endangered?

Help at home

We can do our bit to help animals by thinking about the things we do every day that will help the environment.

Here are some things you can do to help...

Recycle

Plant a tree

Say no to plastic bags

29

Remember

All animals, big and small, are important.

Be kind to animals.

Leave wild animals where you find them.

Good places to see animals are parks, woods and ponds.

Tread carefully when you are looking for nature.

Litter harms wildlife.

We can help endangered animals by cutting back on waste and recycling.

Useful words

Charities   groups of people who work and raise money for those in need

Environment   the natural world

Habitat   a place an animal likes to live

Poaching   hunting an animal for its tusks or fur

Pollution   something that is put out into the natural world that is dirty or that harms it

Recycling   turning something we've used into something new

Shelter   a place that gives protection from weather or danger

Index